Acclaim for The Fundraising Habits of Supremely Successful Boards

"Jerold Panas' advice is crisp and precisely on target. Whether you are a seasoned veteran or brand new to the profession, it will be hard to read this book and not feel energized for the important work we do."

Andrew K. Benton, President
Pepperdine University

"A goldmine of sage advice and compelling anecdotes. *Fundraising Habits* provides the no-nonsense information that trustees need to know and act on if they want to ensure that their board service and its impact are of the highest caliber."

Kolia O'Connor, Head of School
Sewickley Academy

"A book that could only be written by a person who loves people, appreciates the variety and complexity of human nature, and enjoys the challenge of dealing with diversity. Jerold Panas has learned a lot during his multi-faceted career and it is the reader's good fortune that he has the literary skill and the willingness to share his insights with others."

Kermit J. Pike, Chief Operating Officer
Western Reserve Historical Society

"Goes right to the heart of the matter. If you want to help your board develop habits that will lead to superb results in fundraising and fiscal stewardship, this is the book to read and relish."

Dr. Thomas Dillon, President
Thomas Aquinas College

"An overview of boardsmanship at its best. With the wisdom that come from years of experience, Jerold Panas helps every board member of every organization see how they can make a difference."

Dr. Steven G.W. Moore, Sr. Vice President
Asbury Theological Seminary

"An essential guide for every organization aspiring to have a highly-productive board. Motivating and inspiring."

Bruce A. Bartoo, Chief Development Officer
Sisters of Mercy Health System

The Fundraising Habits of Supremely Successful Boards

A 59-Minute Guide to Assuring Your Organization's Future

First printed in June 2006
Printed in the United States of America

ISBN 1-889102-26-1

10 9 8 7 6 5 4 3 2 1

This text is printed on acid-free paper.

> *Copies of this book are available from the*
> *publisher at discount when purchased in*
> *quantity for boards of directors or staff.*

Emerson & Church, Publishers
P.O. Box 338 • Medfield, MA 02052
Tel. 508-359-0019 • www.emersonandchurch.com

Library of Congress Cataloging-in-Publication Data

Panas, Jerold.
  The fundraising habits of supremely successful boards :
a 59-minute guide to ensuring your organization's future /
Jerold Panas.
      p. cm.
  ISBN 1-889102-26-1 (pbk. : alk. paper)
  1. Nonprofit organizations—Finance. 2. Nonprofit
organizations—Management. I. Title.
  HG4027.65.P35 2006
  658.15'224—dc22

                              2006009197

Jerold Panas

The
Fundraising
Habits of
Supremely Successful Boards

A 59-Minute Guide
To Assuring Your
Organization's Future

Emerson
& Church
PUBLISHERS

Also by Jerold Panas

Mega Gifts
Who Gives Them, Who Gets Them,
2nd Edition

Making the Case
The No-Nonsense Guide
to Writing the Perfect Case Statement

ASKING
A 59-Minute Guide to Everything
Board Members, Volunteers, and Staff
Must Know to Secure the Gift

Wit, Wisdom & Moxie
A Compendium of Wrinkles, Strategies,
and Admonitions that Really Work

Finders Keepers
Lessons I've Learned
about Dynamic Fundraising

EXCEL!

Boardroom Verities
A Celebration of Trusteeship

Fundraising Almanac

Born to Raise
What Makes a Fundraiser Great

DEDICATION

This book is dedicated to the millions of board members who give their time, their talent, and, yes, their treasure to noble and great causes.

You cheerful and faithful toilers, you are responsible for changing and saving lives. It could not be done without you.

"We are what we repeatedly do.
Excellence, then, is not an act, but a habit."

– *Aristotle*

CONTENTS

I'D JUMP AT THE CHANCE

I'D JUMP
AT THE CHANCE

◆

"Jay, if the University asked you to call on someone for a gift, would you be willing?"

I'm speaking with Jay Jensen. He's one of the major volunteer leaders at the University of Miami. And one of their most significant donors. In fact, most of his estate is going to the University.

If personality had a color, Jay would be brilliant red. He's effervescent.

"Well, what about it? Would you be willing to ask?"

Not only would he be willing, Jay tells me he'd *love* to do it. "I'd jump at the chance."

When I hear words of such dedication and devotion, my heart soars. A trustee with unbridled passion can move mountains.

"Has anyone from the University ever asked you to call on someone for a gift?" I continue.

"No, never."

Can you believe it, dear reader? No one has ever asked this staunchest of supporters to call on others for a gift.

It got me to thinking about something I've lived by my whole career. My Gospel. It has guided all of my work. *You'll be hurt more by those who would have said, 'yes' but were not asked – than by those who say, 'no.'*

In my work with nearly 2,000 organizations, I find that board members will stand on tiptoes to reach high standards if they know what's expected of them. They will perform extraordinary feats, give unlimited time, combine all their talents for a common and great cause.

But if trustees* don't understand their role, this enormous potential is reduced to a trickle, forced through a narrow institutional funnel.

I see it happen all the time – board members who are waiting for the appropriate charge and challenge. Unfortunately, too many are left waiting.

But not you. You're already giving a part of your life to an organization making a difference. And my hunch is, like Jay Jensen, you're willing to do even more.

Not that it will be easy. There will be times when

---

*Throughout the book, the words "trustees" and "directors" are used interchangeably.

you'll feel like Sisyphus, rolling that boulder up the hill. You never stop because you recognize, as St. Francis said, that the greatest rewards in life come from overcoming difficulties that require "headstrong dedication and magnitude of spirit."

Some of the Habits I describe in this book may make the hill a little less steep, the stone a little lighter. Even so, you'll be plenty challenged.

You have joined a happy and devoted army of over 15 million other men and women in this country who serve on boards.

And just like you, they give selflessly of their time and money to inspiring causes and great institutions. Your organization is winning battles of consequence every day. And it couldn't be done without you.

IT STARTS WITH INTEGRITY

◆

HABIT 1. *In all your actions, integrity rules.*

"Me, I have a fantasy."

That's James Barrett talking. He's on the board of Thomas Aquinas College in California. He's passionate about the College, and backs it up with hard work and sizable gifts.

"I'm at those beautiful pearly gates. St. Peter is peering at me – a long dossier in his hand. After a moment, in a rich baritone, he poses the *big question*: 'What did you do with your life, Jim, that we should let you in?'

"I don't hesitate, not for a second.

"Well, I raised money for a number of important causes," I say. "You know how hard that is."

St. Peter nods.

"I gave away a lot of money, too, I continue."

Another approving nod.

"And integrity and character were always the guiding stars in my personal and professional life.

"The pearly gates swing open. 'Come in, Jim,' says St. Peter. 'We've been expecting you.'"

Like James Barrett, you're willing to raise money for your organization. And just as willing to give generously yourself. But even more important, as a trustee you stand for what is right, even if at times you're standing alone.

It may require courage and high-wire impudence. There are times it can be a scourging test of character. But you don't flinch. Because if you do, you know the reputation of your organization can be easily lost ... forfeited forever. It is the abdication of the institution's spirit and soul.

You identify with Jim Barrett and other trustees like him. You understand that integrity isn't among the most important criteria, it is *the* most important.

Integrity is the thread that binds the organization. And you, a trustee, are the master weaver.

MISSION
IS EVERYTHING

◆

HABIT 2. *You hold in trust the mission of your organization.*

The mission of your organization isn't merely important – it's everything.

It describes your noble objectives and the way you touch the lives of those you serve – in a way unlike any other organization.

Your mission fuels motivation and ignites the passion. It provides the *why* that inspires every *how*. It is the roadmap, the signpost of your organization's direction and destination.

In fact, your mission is the single criterion by which you measure *everything* you do – your programs, your marketing, your financial resources, your hopes and dreams for the future.

In my experience, the most effective trustees are first and foremost models of what I call mission-centered leaders. The mission is their compass. The true North. It points the way.

Like filings to a magnet, these individuals are drawn to an organization because of their interest in its mission. And the longer they serve, the more ingrained and deeply imbedded the mission becomes.

But as committed as trustees are to the mission, they cannot be slaves to it either.

The March of Dimes is a perfect example. Founded in 1938 – the dream of Franklin Delano Roosevelt – the organization's mission was to stop the scourge of polio.

Roosevelt encouraged people everywhere to send in their dimes. And the coins came pouring in.

But then Dr. Jonas Salk developed his polio vaccine in 1955, and the crippling disease was eradicated. The March of Dimes' mission lost its relevancy.

But realizing it could still be a formidable force for good, the organization changed its mission. Today's March of Dimes raises nearly $300 million every year to "improve the health of babies by preventing birth defects, premature birth, and infant mortality." The crusade continues but with a different mission.

There's a moral to the story. No matter how lofty, you cannot hide behind an outdated, groundless mission.

But there's another reason the mission is consequential. It propels your organization's fundraising.

It makes clear who you are – where you're going – and how you plan to get there. It's a dream put into financial action.

Without a consequential mission, you're like a blindfolded kid swinging at a piñata. Your fundraising is hit or miss. Mostly miss.

WHY PEOPLE GIVE

◆

HABIT 3. *You never lose sight that your organization is in the business of changing lives or saving lives.*

Here's a little exercise I like to do. I did it the other day with the national board of Make-A-Wish.

Directors were seated, six to a table. I told them I'd give them 20 minutes to discuss why Make-A-Wish is worthy of receiving gifts. Why might people want to give?

When the time was up, I called on each group for their response. Someone in the front noted every reason on a flipchart.

When all of the groups had reported, there were 89 different reasons! to give.

You would guess some of them: "It gives kids their

last wish." "It's the only organization with our purpose." "People love doing things for kids."

But while the responses were confirming, most didn't quite hit the mark.

From my 40 years of experience, I can say without question the first and foremost reason people give is because your organization changes lives or saves lives.

It is *that* awesome opportunity that inspires them.

Nothing else is as important. Not the memorial opportunity. Not the tax advantage. Not the drama of the project.

A number of other reasons *do* come into play. People give because your programs are relevant. Of course! And have emotional appeal. To be sure! And because of the urgency – yours is a program that can't be put off. There's too much at stake. There are lives to be touched. Now.

But none of these factors, nor your leather-bound proposal or dazzling video, really move donors to their highest possible potential.

No, the touchstone is this: your donors have the power to change a life – save a life. It is through you that they can experience the majesty of giving.

IT DOESN'T JUST HAPPEN

◆

HABIT 4. *You create an atmosphere of excellence.*

Excellence in an organization is never an accident.

When Frances Hesselbein was hired as CEO of the Girl Scouts of the USA, it was the most vulnerable time in the organization's 70-year history.

Membership was in a freefall. Fundraising had plummeted. Budgets were dangerously in the red. Worse, studies showed that members and families felt the program was no longer relevant.

From her very first day, the board made it clear to Hesselbein that changes were needed. They were willing to shake and rattle the status quo. Open up the organization's hardened arteries. And most of all, they wanted to challenge mediocrity. "The board's charge to me," Dr. Hesselbein said, "was to make excellence my creed."

That's how it began. Excellence was invoked from the top, not pushed from the bottom.

In the 14 years Dr. Hesselbein headed Girl Scouts, it grew to be the world's largest organization serving women and girls. Fundraising increased five-fold. Programs were added that breathed new life. And to this day everything from top to bottom is measured against the standard of the highest quality.

None of this would have happened had it not been for the board's determination and commitment to excellence.

I conducted a study a few years back of 100 organizations. The major finding was fascinating. If a board is willing to accept mediocrity in its staff and programs, it almost always gets mediocre staff and programs.

The road to stumbling organizational results is strewn with shoddy work and mediocre staff. Often it's caused by an unthinking adherence to the past, or a reverence for present practices.

Be one with Frances Hesselbein's board – shake and rattle the status quo. Commit to high standards. You'll achieve them before you know it.

ROOM AT THE BOTTOM

◆

HABIT 5. *You continually push for greater success.*

We had just finished a national meeting of The United Way and I'm bold enough to ask Bill Gates about his formula for success.

In essence, he tells me this: Don't be seduced into complacency by a successful operation.

"I'm not good at self-congratulations," he says. "The more successful I am, the more vulnerable I feel."

In other words, when you do something really well, people tend to expect even better results the next time around.

That means you have to work harder and harder

just to hold your position. Remember Alice's admonishment (*Through the Looking Glass*) that you have to run faster and faster just to stay in place.

As a trustee, your job is to make sure everything you do improves and increases the success of your organization.

It's not easy. I liken it to the story of Pablo Casals, considered the greatest cellist who ever lived.

When Casals was celebrating a special birthday, a young reporter asked him: "Mr. Casals, you're now 95 and the greatest cellist who ever lived. Why do you still practice four hours every day?"

"Because I think I'm making progress," answered Casals.

The passion for excellence is a shared responsibility, total dedication on the part of the staff and the board. But it starts with the board.

As a trustee, you understand that past success doesn't ensure future glory. Ten years later, more than a third of the firms appearing in *Fortune 500* no longer exist. Your job is to challenge, shed light with penetrating questions, and burst away the barnacles of present practices with exciting new ideas.

Complacency and even gradual growth are the enemies of organizational vigor and vitality. That's Peter Drucker talking.

There's plenty of room at the bottom for the organization willing to limp along and live on past laurels. Satisfied to operate in the past or to be a me-too, carbon copy of similar organizations.

But that's not for you. You recognize that success is a moving target.

You understand the role of a trustee is to set challenging objectives, establish tight deadlines, and place milestones along the way. You keep raising the bar.

THE COURAGE TO DARE

◆

HABIT 6. *You're willing to leave the Comfort Zone.*

Several years ago, my wife and I worshiped in the majestic Cathedral in Seville, Spain. It was built 400 years ago.

Carved in stone at the building's entrance are the words of Theodore, the Dean of the Cathedral at the time. "Let us build a Cathedral so great that those who follow will think us mad for having made the attempt."

That is what is necessary at times. Trustees have to leave the Comfort Zone – think boldly and take chances.

If Columbus had turned back, no one would have

blamed him. But no one would have remembered him either.

You know the story of Icarus. He flew so close to the sun the wax on his wings melted and he plunged back to earth – from the very brink of achievement to the bowels of failure.

The decline was lamentable. But I wouldn't call it meaningless.

Icarus had seized the moment, experienced a remarkable *high* known to few. Some call it hubris. I side with Robert Browning: "A man's reach should exceed his grasp, or what's a heaven for."

You hear it incessantly. The clatter and clang of those trembling and trepid souls who remind you, "it can't be done." But in today's world, you as a trustee must be willing to erase all the chalk marks. The old guidelines no longer are relevant.

It means asking this question of every decision you make: Does this help us grow? Or does it keep us the way we are?

You can make your institution as great as you wish. It's in your power and province. But it often means leaving the comfort zone. You think audaciously and creatively. You're willing to go out on a limb.

Of course you are. That's where the choicest fruit lie.

A ROARING ADVOCATE

———◆———

HABIT 7. *You're passionate about your organization ... and show it.*

Paige Patterson is president of Southwestern Baptist Seminary. It's the largest seminary in the nation.

I ask Paige what is the single most important characteristic he seeks in a trustee. "Just choose one," I tell him.

There's no hesitation. "I'd ask for passion for my Seminary. I want a trustee who's burning in his bones for the mission here."

I agree with Paige. Trustees with passion make the difference between an organization that is flying or merely flapping its wings.

Money allows your organization to operate. And the commitment of trustees determines what you do. But it is passion that dictates how well you do it.

What we know is that the most important weapon on earth is the human soul on fire. It's what Robert Frost referred to as, "that immense energy of life which sparks a fire."

In a sense, you are an evangelist. You give witness.

If you don't feel fervor for your organization, it may be the wrong cause for you. But if you do, it ignites the fire. The spark from one fire lights another. Soon there is a roaring blaze.

Listen to Paige Patterson. Let your passion for the organization burn like fire in your bones.

DEADLY OFFENSES

◆

HABIT 8. *You maintain a positive attitude.*

With some organizations, if you want to kill an idea, get the board to discuss it. They don't know what they want – and won't be happy until they get it.

I've been a consultant to philanthropy for 40 years. In that time, I've attended hundreds and hundreds of board meetings – perhaps a thousand (surely a sufficient number to earn me a place in heaven on the right hand of the saints and martyrs!).

Time and time again, I've heard the same seven deadly statements that can kill an idea:

"We've never done it that way before."

A board that protects its time-vested interests and its precious heritage blocks the route to change. It is strangled by the *status quo*.

Take a chance. Seize the opportunity. Some decisions require audacious action. It is impossible to be both consistently bold and infallible.

"It can't be done."

In these times of explosive change and extraordinary complexity, to say *impossible* always puts you on the losing side. An organization harboring the attitude, "it can't be done," has signed-off on a self-fulfilling promise of failure.

If you believe it can be done – it can. This must be the hymn you sing.

"It'll cost too much."

Not having funds is a temporary problem ... surrounded by creative solutions. To say you have insufficient funds for objectives of consequence bespeaks lowly aspirations.

You hold in trust the mission of your organization and the responsibility for its funding. That is a commitment to be faithfully sustained with unrelenting resolve and intrepid dedication.

Resources must not determine decisions. Your decisions determine resources.

"We've been doing all right without it."

It was Will Rogers who said: "Even if you're on the

right tra   e."

Tho   will
eventu   and
already   yard.

"W   ."

As   it be"
rather   past.
Even the   piring
opportunity when pursued with a belief in the *possible*.
Or as Clement Stone, the father of positive thinking,
colorfully put it: "You've got a problem. Great!"

"We're not ready now."

If not now – when?
TNT must be your creed – Today Not Tomorrow.
Move forward and make your decision with a
symphony of hard work, persistence, and unwavering
commitment.

"Let's put it off for now and discuss it later."

Indecision is contagious. It casts an unhealthy pall
over each member of the board.
Ross Perot contends that too often an organization
says: "ready, aim, aim, aim, aim." Perot recommends
instead the concept: "Ready, fire, aim."
The theory is valid. Most often, it is far better to

take action even though all the factors may not be known, than to take no action at all.

•••

The other day, while waiting in the doctor's office, I came across an article in an old issue of *National Geographic*.

You'll laugh when I tell you the subject – barnacles. But one fascinating paragraph stayed with me.

"The barnacle," this article said, "is confronted early on with a decision about where it is going to live. Once it decides that, it spends the rest of its life with its head permanently cemented to a rock."

For some boards, it does come to that!

Thankfully you know better.

THE FUTURE ISN'T WHAT IT USED TO BE

---◆---

HABIT 9. *You plan.*

The great failing of many organizations isn't in missing goals and objectives. It lies in not setting any to reach. Failing to reach the stars is no cause for shame. Not standing on tiptoes to grasp for them is.

A strategic plan is a dream with a deadline. And your role as a trustee is to help formulate one.

Some organizations are like Jack Kerouac's characters in *On the Road.*

"We got to go and never stop going until we get there."

"But where are we going, man?"

"I don't know, but we got to go."

39

A strategic plan allows your organization to create its future. You decide where you want to be five years from now, 10 years – and you determine how to get there.

The Wadley Blood Center in Dallas was one of the largest and most respected in the country. There was a time when it served all of Dallas, most of Texas, and was a reservoir for special blood needs across the nation.

The Center was well funded, had a regular stream of blood donors, and was highly regarded by Dallas and its leadership. It was considered an indispensable community asset.

At a board meeting I attended, the CEO suggested that because Wadley was dominant in the country, it should launch a program immediately to conduct cancer research.

"We know so much about blood, and have such a large supply, it will be easy for us to move right into research," the CEO said. He told the group it would cost about $25 million to begin the program. This could easily be done from reserves and annual operations.

The board was split. I remember Herbert Hunt (one of the Hunt brothers) was vehemently against it. "This is ridiculous," he said. "Who did the planning?"

Hunt continued his objection. "Why are we moving into cancer research anyway? Our mission is blood."

Someone suggested they undertake a strategic plan.

Those in favor of moving forward with the research said such a plan would take too long. There wasn't time. Some said they didn't need it. A few even said it would cost too much (ironic since these same people were willing, with little study, to undertake a $25 million! project).

On a split vote, the board decided to proceed with the cancer research. Wadley plunged ahead. No plan, no guidelines, no restraints.

In no time at all, the Center burned through all of its reserves. At the same time, perhaps because of its split objectives, Wadley began losing its share of the blood market. Little by little at first, then suddenly the blood supply plummeted.

Several years ago, the Wadley Blood Center went out of business.

There's a lesson here. No plan, no future. If you don't have a roadmap, you won't know where you're going or how to get there.

Strategic planning, says Peter Drucker, doesn't deal with future decisions. It defines the future of present decisions. As a trustee, your job is to have a blind date with destiny.

AVOID MEDDLING

◆

HABIT 10. *You don't manage the operation.*

Randall Meyer is never in doubt. When he speaks, you want to carve the words in stone.

Meyer is former president and CEO of the Exxon Company.

He has served on several notable boards. These include his alma mater, the University of Iowa; the Methodist Hospital in Houston, one of the largest medical centers in America; and MD Anderson, the premiere cancer treatment center in the world.

"It's the way I pay back for the good life I've had," Randy says of his service.

As a result of his wealth of board experience, Randy is emphatic on one issue. Board members shouldn't get involved in the management of the operation. If a trustee feels the organization is ill-managed, you deal with the Chief Executive Officer. To do otherwise is counter-productive, he says.

Randy said something else that leaves an indelible mark on me. "To be an effective board member, you don't manage more, you *demand* more."

The word "demand" may bother some. I think Randy used it to underline his point. He meant that as a board member, you require more, you expect more.

That's your job as a trustee – to keep raising the bar. More members, more donors, more programs, more service – all driven by quality and an intense focus on mission.

But you don't get involved in management. Period!

Determining policy is the province of the board and the board only. *Executing* policy is the responsibility of staff.

The CEO leads. The staff designs and implements. And the board empowers.

If trustees attempt to manage, it places the organization in disarray and impedes its growth. The staff sees that things are done right. The board sees that the right things are done.

Ahh, the temptation may be great at times to meddle. But you resist!

PASS IT ON

◆

HABIT 11. *You're constantly on the lookout for key people to join the board.*

The Burnham Institute (La Jolla, California) is one of the leading research centers in America. There are 600 researchers and scientists bound in a common crusade to find the cure for a number of diseases that afflict the world.

At this very minute, the Institute is working feverishly to unlock the mystery of curing cancer.

When I met with the board, I said something that came as a surprise to some: "You're as important in conquering cancer as any of the scientists here. Why? Because you provide the advocacy, the passion, and the funding that make it happen."

The same can be said of you. If you're on the board

of a college, you're every bit as important as any dean or faculty member. Or if yours is a hospital board, the physicians and nurses couldn't do their job without you. Count the symphony in there, too. You're just as central to its success as the great maestro.

It couldn't be done without you.

Small wonder you're proud to be a part of your organization's work and service. "The richness of the human journey is here. Observe. Listen. Pass it on," said Bruno Bettelheim.

And that's one of your important responsibilities – to pass it on. To seek out like-minded individuals who will commit themselves to the cause.

You can't leave this solely to the Nominating Committee or the Committee on Board Management. It is the job of every trustee.

My decades of experience convinces me that there's a world of friends (they may not yet know they are friends!) willing to serve on your board. They're just waiting to be asked.

I think of James Gamble. He's the grandson of the founder of Proctor & Gamble and a generous donor to many important causes. Someone on the Nominating Committee at Scripps College (Claremont, California) suggested him for the board. I was at the meeting.

Most of those present said he'd be a priceless asset but would never serve. Don't even bother to ask, some said. The meeting was filled with naysayers. He doesn't know the College. He's too busy. He spends much of the year away from his home in Pasadena.

But one trustee persisted and Gamble was approached. You know what's coming next. He accepted. What a coup for the college!

It's not always easy. The competition is fierce. Recruiting the most capable board members possible requires the same level of cultivation and romancing as does a major gift.

And in truth, the "right trustee" *is* a major gift – of a different kind. He or she is further assurance of your organization's ultimate success.

That's why it's crucial to spend whatever time needed in the search and enlistment process. It is your board's most important priority – and one of your foremost responsibilities as a trustee.

Harriet Beecher Stowe said, "To be involved in a cause of truly great significance is a virtue so noble as to be worthy of canonization."

You are a trustee. Ask others to join you in this Lordly cause. Pass it on.

THE RIGHT STUFF

◆

HABIT 12. *You strive to recruit trustees
with the 4Ws.*

Work. Wealth. Wisdom. These are the 3 Ws you
seek and hope for in a board member. I've added a
fourth, which I'll explain in a moment. Let me first
tell you about the genesis of the 3Ws.

Dr. Henry Wriston ended a distinguished 18-year
presidency at Brown University in 1955. It was a good
school when he was first installed, but not really
distinguished. It was Dr. Riston who developed Brown
into what it is today – one of the elite universities in
America.

When he retired, a reporter from the *Boston Globe*
asked Dr. Riston if there was any secret to his
extraordinary tenure and long roster of achievements.

"It has something to do with vision and leadership," he said. "And the willingness to dare and take on programs others considered impossible. But what is by far most important of all is that through the years, I worked with an outstanding board of trustees."

Following up, the reporter then asked Riston what a president should expect of a trustee.

"I don't need much time to think about that. I would say: Work, Wealth, and Wisdom. Preferably, I want all three. But if I must, I would settle for a minimum of two out of the three."

That formula has stood the test of time.

An organization needs trustees who are willing to *work*, to put in the hours, attend committee meetings, review financial statements, and endure long (at times overly long!) board reports. As the Gospel writer Luke said: "the Lord loves those who serve."

And, of course, you want trustees who bring mature judgment to very complex matters. You need the best minds possible, wise enough to make the right decisions (often on the spot). You look for *wisdom*.

And *wealth*! Ahh! You need those who are willing and able to make sacrificial gifts. You seek trustees who will stretch, who will make your organization the focus of their greatest philanthropy.

And now for the fourth W (my contribution, if I may say so). You want men and women with *Wallop*. Read that: clout, power, and leverage.

You want trustees with influence within their own community and among your constituency. People who can open doors. Attract other leaders to the cause. Serve as ambassadors to others of influence.

Use these Ws to measure your own contribution to the organization. And let them be the guidepost for recruiting other members to your board.

There is actually a fifth W I should mention.

Recently, I was discussing the 4Ws with the Board of the American Red Cross. Mclanie Sabelhaus, a member of the board and chair of the United Way campaign in Baltimore, shot up her hand to interrupt me.

"There's one more W," she exclaims to the group. "Women!"

Absolutely. Women now control nearly 60 percent of the nation's net worth. And that number is growing each year. You had better make certain you have a strong representation of women on your board.

As a trustee, you are a beacon. Seek others who will follow your light. Offer them a promissory note for what can be a great and fulfilling adventure.

I've heard it said that on Judgment Day, the first question you are asked is: Did you return in life all you were given? Serving on a board is a singular way of paying back.

YOU INVEST

◆

HABIT 13. *The organization whose board you serve on is among your top philanthropic priorities.*

Paul Folino is Chair of the Performing Arts Center in Orange County, California. Recently we had a conversation about the importance of board members giving to their organizations.

What Paul tells me may surprise you.

"Here, the stated expectation is $50,000 a year," he says. "If they can't meet that, they're asked to serve in some other capacity, perhaps on a committee."

I'm incredulous. "Do you mean every trustee gives $50,000 a year?"

"Yes they do," he says emphatically.

But that's not all. Paul says each trustee is expected

to *bring in* at least that much from others in the county.

"We follow the dictum: *Give, Get, or Get off*!"

My first thought is, Good grief, you must have trouble recruiting trustees. But as I learn from Paul, there's actually a waiting list. Imagine – people lining up to give $50,000!

What has happened is that by raising the bar, there's a certain social caché to belonging to the board of the Performing Arts Center. It's considered an honor. I'm reminded of what Groucho Marx said: "I'd never belong to a club that would have me as a member."

In your own particular organization, $50,000 may be too high. But don't let the figure scare you. I know of many organizations where the expected level of trustee giving is $10,000. For others it's $5,000. Many are even lower. But the Performing Arts Center example does forcibly deliver the point: as a board member, you must give.

Especially if you hope to get!

Judy Jolley Mohraz, who heads the Virginia G. Piper Charitable Trust, the largest foundation in Arizona, makes that very clear.

"We wouldn't consider a grant to an organization if the directors weren't 100% in their giving. Why would we? If they don't care enough for their organization to give to it, why should we?"

This isn't unusual. We find most foundations now look carefully at board giving. And for some, it's not even a matter of 100% participation. They want to examine whether some directors are giving to their potential.

The late Peter F. Drucker remains one of the most significant voices in management and organizational structure. His superb book for nonprofits should be considered required reading (*Managing the Non-Profit Organization*, 1990, HarperCollins).

Drucker points out that the primary and most important constituency in fund development at any institution is its own board. "It begins with the family."

It's no longer enough that a board simply be in sympathy with the organization and give time. Those are givens and represent a characterization of what Drucker calls the old-type board.

"In today's world, you need a board that takes an active lead in giving and raising money," he says. "I can't imagine a board member who cares greatly about his or her institution not making a significant gift."

Claremont-McKenna College (California) has a brilliant way of helping trustees understand their responsibility in giving. Their minimum gift is expected to be a student's tuition (now $41,000 a year). Thomas Mitchell, chair of the College's Advancement Committee, tells me most trustees give more than that.

Don't worry if your organization's level is lower than this. But aim high. Ask trustees to stand on tiptoes.

Trustees who fail to give place their organization in manacles – forged and fashioned of a rigid spirit and lowly aspirations.

Martin Luther said God divided the hand into fingers so the money would slip through to worthy causes. As a trustee, you must spread your fingers wide!

TWICE BLESSED

◆

HABIT 14. *You ask others to give.*

"Before they join the board, we let directors know they're expected to call on others for gifts. It's part of their responsibility. And we take that seriously."

That's Vicki Weaver talking. She's the Chief Development Officer for Spectrum Health, one of the largest healthcare providers in Michigan.

I ask what happens with directors who tell her they don't like to ask – or say they simply can't ask.

"I hear that all the time," Vicki tells me. "Or worse, they say they don't like to beg.

"But I tell them it's not begging. I'm emphatic about that. I tell them the money they raise helps save lives.

"I also let them know they don't have to make any call alone. I'm willing to go with them on all visits. Or

I'll team them up with another board member."

Hear, too, what DonnaLee Holton says. She's chair of the Helen DeVos Children's Hospital Foundation (Grand Rapids, Michigan), which is launching one of the largest campaigns ever undertaken for a children's hospital.

"When I took over as chair," DonnaLee says, "I knew I had to set the pace with asking. I wanted to be a model for our directors.

"Not everyone on a board is capable of making a large gift. But everyone is able and should be expected to call on others for gifts."

Michael Bloomberg is yet another advocate. You probably know him best of all as Mayor of New York.

He's also one of the most significant philanthropists in the country. His gifts to Johns Hopkins (his *alma mater*) alone have totaled well over $200 million.

Bloomberg tells me that because of the size of his gifts, he is almost always called on by a board member. "I expect that. I think that's an important job of a trustee. I'm on some boards and I consider it my responsibility to ask for gifts."

As busy as he is, I ask how he finds time to solicit gifts. "I don't find time," he says. "I make time."

Most institutions don't lack a culture of philanthropy. They lack a culture of asking.

But something terrible happens when trustees fail

to call on others. Nothing! It's amazing what you don't raise when you don't ask.

A gift to your institution is twice blessed. It blesses those who give. And it blesses those who ask.

BACK TO THE WELL

◆

HABIT 15. *You realize that those who give are your best donors for the future.*

"You can't keep going back to the same well," declared the trustee.

I was at a board meeting recently at an independent school in western Pennsylvania. One of the board members was adamant: they couldn't keep going back to the same old donors.

And in truth this is a well-worn maxim. It's as old as fundraising itself, repeated often, and usually with the same satisfying finality as a Bach cantata.

The only trouble ... it's absolutely untrue. A hoary saw that's totally baseless.

You can indeed keep going back to the well. As a

matter of fact, that's where your greatest potential is.

It's as simple as this: giving begets giving. The more a person gives, the more she keeps giving. And giving.

What's really difficult is getting someone to give who has never given before. Or worse, has no philanthropic intent and gives to nothing.

Take Thomas, for instance, in Champaign, Illinois. For years, he made the *Forbes'* list as one of the wealthiest men in the country.

When we were working with the University of Illinois Library, everyone insisted we put him on the prospect list. One of the board members said: "Heck, Tom could do the whole darn campaign himself."

Well, indeed, he could have ... with nary a blip in his net worth. The trouble is, he had never given to the University. In fact, as far as we could tell, he had never given to anything.

We should certainly call on him, but I didn't harbor much hope. It's what Samuel Johnson said about marrying the same woman twice – it's a case of faith over experience.

Whereas a group like the Mormons (Church of Jesus Christ of Latter-day Saints) *are* reliable prospects for giving – especially to another Mormon project. Members are obligatory tithers, a minimum of 10 percent of gross income to the Church. Many are double-tithers. Their generosity is boundless and they give to countless worthy causes. Their well never runs dry.

If you want the real maxim, here it is: *Givers give.* Which explains why at the end of your campaign if you're short of goal, you call on those who have already given. You don't go to those who earlier said, "call on me later." Chances are they'll put you off again.

Your organization needs financial support. As a board member you're willing to ask others for it. You need to know you can indeed go back to the well.

Follow one of Pope John Paul's last Encyclics to his Bishops: "Go deep, go deeper, go deeper still."

Beware The Trojan Horse

---◆---

HABIT 16. *You understand that not all gifts are worth accepting.*

Not all gifts are what they seem.

We were in the middle of a campaign at The Asheville School (North Carolina) and had reached that point where we needed something big to happen. Something consequential.

We had gotten off to a great start. The board had given sacrificially. A number of major gifts had come in just at the level we hoped. But now we were stalled. Little was happening. And it was painful.

Then Peter calls (you would recognize his real name immediately). He wants to give $7 million! We were singing the doxology.

There was only one hitch. Peter wanted the money to be used to reestablish the small campus lake he remembered when he was a student.

Filled in years ago, the lake had been a maintenance problem and a worrisome safety risk – students loved going swimming at midnight. (That's what Peter seemed to remember most about his days at Asheville!) Now there was an inviting meadow on the spot.

Peter wanted the lake back. And if it costs a little more than the $7 million, he'll up his gift, he tells us.

A special meeting of the board was called. Restoring the lake wasn't part of the campaign. Nor did it figure in any future plans. After hours of discussion, the board decided to go back to Peter and ask if his proposed gift could be diverted to another purpose.

But Peter was insistent. He wanted the lake. And he'd pay for the engineering fees if that was a problem. He also made it clear – no lake, no gift ... of *any* size.

Another all-day special board meeting. Maybe it would be nice to have the lake again, one trustee mused. A few others agreed. "It *was* a popular spot." But in the end, the board did the right thing. They refused the gift.

Trustees like you and those at the Asheville School have a responsibility to determine what gifts might compromise the organization. And believe me, there's plenty of precedent to guide you.

Take the $20 million that Lee Bass, an alumnus, gave to Yale University. He wanted the school to expand its offerings in Western Civilization. A virtuous and noble cause. There was only one provision.

Lee also wanted to name the professors who would benefit from the gift. After four years of agonizing debate, the eye-popping sum was returned. You can't make a gift, no matter the size, and expect to hold the institution hostage.

At other times, the right decision isn't so clear.

I was at a board meeting at Pacific Union College (Angwin, California). Trustees were split evenly about accepting a sizable gift from a local winery. The College is Seventh-day Adventist and Adventists are adamantly anti-alcohol. It's one of the church's inflexible tenets.

I watched as Trustees moved to one end of the room or the other to show their position. From both sides, the arguments grew heated and vehement. The chair was having trouble maintaining control. Forget about decorum!

Finally, someone said: "Malcolm, you've been quiet the whole time. What do you think about this?" Malcolm was the highly respected president of the University.

The moment was suddenly flooded with thundering silence.

"Well," said Malcolm, "I think the devil has had this money long enough. I believe it's time we had it for our use."

That's all it took. Trustees voted to accept the gift, and as one board member said "with deep appreciation to the wonders of the Lord."

You may be familiar with John Steinbeck's wonderful novel, *The Pearl.* In it, a poor Mexican fisherman discovers a pearl in one of his oysters. But instead of leading to happiness and treasures, it brings him only envy among his friends and neighbors. And violence to his family. He discovers he can't even convert his find to ready cash. The pearl turns out to be no gift at all.

Well, life can be like that. And trustees are expected to make the hard decisions. What you thought held great promise may turn out to be no gift at all.

HEARTFELT THANKS

◆

HABIT 17. *You're involved in acknowledging and thanking donors.*

One of the largest medical centers in the country was having a severe problem with attrition. They were hemorrhaging donors.

To find out why, we were engaged to study the situation.

What we learned was distressing. Thirty-four percent of last year's donors said they didn't remember making a gift. And 27 percent told us they didn't feel their gift was important. Small wonder that donors weren't renewing.

What a failing. I'm sure acknowledgments were sent out, but as for showing proper appreciation, that's another story.

Make certain this doesn't happen in your organization.

Not only is it good manners to thank donors, it's fiscally prudent. It costs a whopping 4 1/2 times the resources, staff, and energy to acquire a new donor as it does to keep a current one.

You can be sure that if donors to this medical center had been thanked in a genuine way, they would have remembered making their gift. And they wouldn't have questioned its importance to the organization and those it serves.

Today's donors are often skeptical and unsentimental. Yes, they care about the organization. But they want to know the results of their gifts. Who benefited and how? And properly acknowledging their gifts is the first step of what they see as organizational accountability.

These donors see their gifts as an "investment." And they want to make certain their investment is paying dividends.

For the organization willing to extend itself beyond the typical receipt and form letter (Stuart Irby, in Jackson Mississippi, would wet his thumb and run it over the signature to see if it was individually signed), these times offer an extraordinary opportunity to stand out from other organizations.

And as a trustee you have a role here. In fact, there's nothing quite so memorable for a donor as a board member taking the time to call and say thank you. At the very least, send a personal letter.

I had a role in getting Board members of the Salvation Army in Omaha, Nebraska to follow up on a $100 gift that came through the mail. The phone call was made ... that resulted in a visit to the bachelor's home ... that in the end produced a $3 million gift!

I won't promise that large a gift with every call, but if you wish to retain your donors year after year, if you would like them to increase their giving – get involved. Call to thank them. Celebrate their gift.

BEING THERE

◆

HABIT 18. *You attend board meetings.*

"I need a record of your board attendance," Curt Meadows tells me.

At the time, he was president of the Meadows Foundation, one of the largest in Texas.

I had just presented Curt with a preliminary proposal.

"Perfect," he says. "Precisely what we're interested in." (I'm doing mental high-fives.)

"Send me your final proposal and a certified copy of your board attendance for the last 18 months."

I'm thinking: Eighteen months? Certified?

"Why would you want that," I ask, as nonchalantly as I can.

Curt tells me if the attendance isn't at least

75 percent, I don't even have to worry about sending a proposal. The Foundation won't consider a grant.

At first blush, I thought this was overly severe. Cripes! That's a demanding test.

I've since come to realize it's entirely appropriate. If board members don't think enough of the organization to attend meetings, why should a Foundation (or any funder for that matter) consider a gift?

Mrs. William H. Gates, Sr. (Bill's mother!) was a member of the national board of the United Way. In all her time serving, she never missed one quarterly meeting. Moreover, she was there for all specially called gatherings as well as those of the two committees she served on. I asked her about her perfect attendance.

"You crossed the country, Seattle to Washington and back, dozens of times. You never missed a meeting. Is that simply part of your nature?"

"Yes," Mrs. Gates told me, "but it's more than that. If I join a board, I feel I'm obligated to attend. If I miss a meeting, I haven't played my role."

Attending meetings is the only way you can effectively track the status and progress of the institution. And monitor the quality. Mrs. Gates makes the point quite clearly. "I'm here to reject the mediocre."

Most board decisions affect finances and fundraising. That makes attendance particularly important.

There's one thing more. Poor attendance at a meeting is demoralizing. It calls into question the board's interest and commitment. "I need to attend." Mrs. Gates told me, "to bring unity and spirit."

One of Albert Einstein's favorite sayings was: "Not everything that counts can be counted. And not everything that can be counted counts." In this instance I can assure you that your board attendance is counted. And it counts.

DO YOUR HOMEWORK

◆

HABIT 19. *You're prepared for every meeting you attend.*

For the past 20 years, Martha Ingram has been involved with every significant project in Nashville. And her influence spreads far beyond the city.

She has chaired a dozen major organizations, including Vanderbilt University. Her family gift to Vanderbilt is the largest ever in this country to an institution of higher learning.

But her great passion is music and particularly the Nashville Symphony. She now heads the $200 million campaign for Nashville's new Center for the Performing Arts. The goal will be reached – and a lot of it will come from Martha herself. She'll also make most of the calls for the largest gifts.

There's something that really upsets this dynamic woman. And that's when trustees come to board meetings unprepared.

"On the boards I chair," Martha tells me, "we spend a lot of time gathering material for trustees to review in advance of the meeting. We need their wisdom. We wouldn't have them on the board if we didn't."

So when trustees come to a meeting, Martha expects them to be fully armed – with questions and the willingness to discuss and debate.

Think for a moment of the collective wisdom and repository of experience gathered around the board table. It is an unforgiving failure if trustees come to a meeting unprepared

One thing I'm sure. No trustee of a board Martha chairs ever comes to a *second* meeting unprepared.

Take a cue from this exemplary volunteer. Whether you're debating the launch of a multi-million dollar campaign or an after-school program for latchkey kids, acquaint yourself with the issue and come fully prepared to contribute.

After all, you hold in your hands the organization's future. You are its destiny.

YOU WORRY

---◆---

HABIT 20. *You take your fiduciary role seriously.*

Recall Wilkins Micawber, the incurable optimist in David Copperfield. He lives on the precipice of ruin. But always he reassures himself, and those around him, not to worry – because "something surely will turn up."

You know better. You are a trustee. Your charge is to worry!

At Eckerd College (Florida) several years ago, it was discovered that the Chief Financial Officer was dipping into the (restricted) endowment to balance the budget. Serious dipping.

I know that board. I've worked with them. You couldn't possibly find a more committed and devoted group of trustees.

They simply weren't watching the financials. Neither was the president. He was totally innocent.

The financial officer was fired and the president, who felt a responsibility as the chief executive officer, took early retirement. It took a $40 million campaign conducted in 60 days to replace the funds.

As a trustee, the funds and finances of the institution are in your trust (that's why *trustee* is such an empowering word for your role).

Among other things, this means you insist on easy to understand financial statements and review them regularly.

It also means that before authorizing annual operating budgets or major capital expenditures – something only you can do – you understand the budgeting process and ask plenty of questions.

There are times you may find the financial statement difficult to understand. An aggregation of muddle! But you probe. Because you know it's your responsibility to be uneasy and meticulous stewards of the funds.

In short, you worry!

WEAR YOUR BUSINESS HAT

---◆---

HABIT 21. *You exercise sound business judgment.*

I couldn't believe I was actually picking up the phone to make the call. (But I always admonish my clients to never say 'no' for anyone.)

I was calling information. "Please give me the telephone number for Peter Drucker in Claremont, California."

(The nerve!)

"Do you wish Peter F. Drucker on Wellesley Drive?" she asks.

"Yes, yes please," I tell her. (How many Peter Druckers can there be in Claremont?)

"The number is 714 ....

I still have my pencil notes. The year was 1988.

Dr. Drucker answers in a thick Viennese brogue. I work with a number of nonprofit organizations, I tell him. I know he works with corporations all over the world and I'm wondering if there's any similarity at all with nonprofits. I ask if I might visit him sometime.

To my complete surprise, the next words out of Dr. Drucker's mouth are: "Can you come on a Sunday?"

Before I know it, we make a date. I find my way to Wellesley Drive. I'm met by Peter Drucker in shirtsleeves and no tie. He ushers me into his modest house and directs me to a little breakfast area off the kitchen.

At the time, Dr. Drucker was working on a book about the principles of managing a nonprofit. That's why he was willing to see me, he says – to bounce some ideas off me. (Peter Drucker wanting to bounce ideas off me. Oh sure!) I ask if I might take notes.

We talked for nearly two hours that day and it was fascinating. I could fill two books with his insights, but what's relevant here are a few things Dr. Drucker was adamant about.

"I would put a big sign in every boardroom that says: 'Use good business judgment and the money will follow.'" That's where it starts, he emphasized – with proper business principles. "That takes the right thinking on the part of directors."

And keep your focus on results. While there's virtue to a board that works hard, results are what count, said Dr. Drucker. Heed these next words: "Results come from exploiting opportunities, not from solving problems. Put all of your resources and thinking into opportunities, not into problems."

Jack Welch once told a group: "At General Electric we never talk about problems. We only talk about opportunities. But there are times we have a hell of a lot of opportunities."

Let me tell you about two colleges that had a lot of "opportunities"!

This is a case of two boards in almost identical situations making totally different decisions. Both were right for their institutions, and both were wrenching decisions for trustees.

Hood College (Frederick, Maryland) was founded in 1893. For over 100 years it was a women's college of prestige and stature. But as the late 1990s approached, it found itself, like many other all-women's colleges, in severe difficulty.

Declining enrollment, inadequate fundraising, deferred maintenance, and buildings in need of renovation. But academically, it was superb.

The board was faced with a tangled dilemma. It could continue on and face the possible dire consequences. Or it could consider going coeducational.

Most boards at one time or another face the question: are we willing to do whatever it takes? There would be many of Hood's alumnae who would be plenty upset if the College became co-ed. No doubt some would end their support.

At the same time the board reasoned: if we prepare properly, we can greatly increase the enrollment. And if we tell the story effectively and make the case, we can measurably increase our fundraising.

The board opted to go co-ed. Their situation has dramatically improved. And Hood College is now powered by an extremely efficient president and a board with an abiding commitment.

And now consider Cedar Crest, a women's college in Allentown, Pennsylvania. About the same age as Hood.

Cedar Crest was facing decreased enrollment and an even steeper decline in the fundraising. Despite its quality education and highly touted faculty, there was a question of survival.

About a dozen years ago, several on the board came up with what appeared to be a perfect solution. Cedar Crest would merge with Muhlenberg College, also in Allentown.

Discussions began and the marriage was nearly consummated. But the bride said "no" at the altar!

When the time came for a final vote, a majority of

trustees were adamant. The College would remain all women. They were convinced there was a place in higher education for a college with the qualities and mission of Cedar Crest.

Several trustees resigned immediately, but the college didn't die. Quite the contrary.

A new president was hired, someone fully dedicated to education for women. Dorothy Gulbenkian Blaney began running from the very day she arrived. And has never stopped. She brought enthusiasm and energy. Her passion was infectious.

The board deepened its commitment. Alumni responded as never before. Enrollment climbed. Fundraising doubled. And Cedar Crest thrives today.

Two colleges, similar in size and character. Both with similar issues. And both blessed with trustees willing to deliberate and make business decisions that were complex and onerous. And both decisions were right for their particular institution.

St. Basil perhaps said it best: "No one who shuns the blows and dust of battle wins a crown."

HUSBANDS
THE FUNDS

◆

HABIT 22. *You monitor the investments.*

Husbands – that's not a verb you hear often these days.

But its meaning is precisely what I have in mind. To conserve, preserve, manage, and watch over. One definition I saw went even further: to husband is "to count the pennies"!

The Harvard Class of 1954 celebrated its 50th Anniversary in a rather remarkable way. They presented Harvard with gift of $90 million. It's an impressive amount, but the story behind it is even more fascinating.

Forty years before, when alumni were celebrating

their 10th Anniversary, they heard from the treasurer of the College. The report chronicled horrendous results of the College's investments. It was dreadful and embarrassing.

The class decided they could improve on this. And they took action.

The group – 15 alumni in all – decided to ante up $10,000 each. They would invest this $150,000. And while there were some pretty savvy investors among the group, they decided to hire a professional as well.

In truth, Harvard officials were never crazy about the idea. These alumni had incorporated as an independent 501(c)3. On more than a few occasions, the University asked the group to release the funds. But the Class refused.

Over the years, the investment grew. And grew. On their 50th Anniversary, the Class of 1954 was able to turn over a tidy sum. Are you ready? The $150,000 had grown to $90 million. What an extraordinary class gift!

I don't for a minute suggest you establish an autonomous 501(c)3. But what I do recommend is that you carefully and regularly review the reserves and endowment of your organization. You need to know how effectively the funds are invested and how well the corpus is growing.

We worked with a small college in Oklahoma. The Mabee Foundation had been funding them generously for years. We assumed our request for the new science building would be easily accepted.

Mabee turned us down.

When the Foundation discovered the College had been earning less than two percent the last three years on its investments, they said the trustees had not exercised proper fiduciary responsibility. "You have not been good stewards of your funds," they wrote.

You can't duck this fiscal responsibility. Even if you don't serve on the Finance or Investment Committee, you are accountable.

You are a *trustee*. The funds have been placed in your trust.

KEEP AN EYE
ON THE FAT BOY

◆

HABIT 23. *You're keenly aware of the
competition.*

Jascha Heifetz is considered the greatest violinist this country ever produced. When he made his American debut at Carnegie Hall, the audience was filled with musicians eager to hear this 15-year-old protégé whose reputation had glowingly preceded him.

The renowned concert violinist Mischa Elman, was there. Soon after Heifetz began, Elman leaned over to his companion, the pianist Leopold Todowsky: "It's getting hot in here, isn't it?" he whispered. "Not for pianists," Todowsky replied.

Competition can be plenty tough.

The fact that it's difficult to see the signs doesn't mean they aren't there. It's up to you as a trustee – as someone close to the pulse of your community or constituency – to recognize and understand the signals. And take action.

The road of institutional failure is paved with organizations satisfied with past achievements. An unremarkable, standstill present. Not vigilant to the growth of similar institutions.

You want to be *Primus Inter Pares* – first among equals. If you don't compare, you face the possibility of being overtaken – much like Mike Campbell in *The Sun Also Rises*: "Gradually ... then all of a sudden."

When Dean Rusk was running the Rockefeller Foundation, he advised his staff and board to keep an eye on the Ford Foundation. "What the fat boy in the canoe does makes a difference to everybody else," he said.

ASK FOR HELP

◆

HABIT 24. *You call upon a consultant when necessary.*

Bob was terribly excited when he called. "I'm going to ask Dale for $25 million for the new Cardiac Center. I'm taking Peter with me."

Here's the cast. Bob is an effective fundraiser in an eastern Pennsylvania hospital. He's completely unafraid of asking. Dale has a very high net worth and has just undergone an intricate heart operation. Peter is the surgeon who completed the successful operation.

Everything for this call was perfect. Well, nearly so.

Taking the physician is a master stroke. No one gives more than a grateful patient. And giving to the new heart center should have great appeal for Dale.

It's the size of the gift that gnaws. Asking for too much can backfire. It can draw a negative – even angry – response at times.

"How did you come up with $25 million?" I ask.

"I just think it's the right amount. He's got plenty of money."

"Has he been giving to the hospital?" I gently press. Bob tells me he hasn't been much of a donor.

"Has he ever made a large gift to any other organization you know about? Maybe his alma mater or the museum campaign in town?"

"Not that I'm aware of," says Bob.

You're probably ahead of me on this. You would have counseled patience. "Bob, everything is in place but the amount. You have the right caller. The motivation to give to a heart-oriented program seems appropriate. But you have no way of knowing about the amount." That's what you would have said.

I tell Bob he needs to do a lot of probing on this first call – to see this visit as an exploratory one. We call these *discovery visits*. There are a lot of questions that need to be answered. It's too soon to ask for a gift – especially at the level he's thinking.

I suggest to Bob four or five questions to ask the prospective donor. And I tell him what's most important is to listen, not talk. Probe, ask, listen.

Another time, for an independent school, I spoke with an alumnus who was evaluated by the staff as a

$1 million prospect. In my visit with the donor, I discovered he had made several gifts of $5 million to other organizations. He also told me the school had changed his life.

We decided to ask for $5 million. And got it.

At times like I've described here, an outside voice can be critical. It can affect your bottom line dramatically – spelling the difference between token sums and multi-million dollar gifts.

A consultant can help set direction, monitor progress, and raise the organization's bar. A consultant can also speak convincingly and with authority to trustees.

At a Midwest YMCA recently, the CEO took me aside after the board meeting. "Hey, you told them what I've been saying for months – and they listened to you and agreed." Bingo! An "outside voice" speaks loudly.

No Money, No Mission

◆

HABIT 25. *You don't allow a mission deficit.*

The financial strength of your organization is important for all the reasons you know – but especially from a fundraising standpoint. No one wants to give to an organization with financial woes, to save the sinking Titanic.

If you've been balancing your budget, yours is among the fortunate organizations – well-managed and with good board oversight.

But what if you're perched precariously on the precipice, challenged each year to make ends meet. It can be a steep, slippery slope. Ah, that's the static that crackles.

Balancing the budget can be done in two ways. You can either reduce your costs or increase your revenue. The latter is always the preferable way.

Oh, sure – eliminate unnecessary expenses. Cut the fat. But your responsibility as a trustee is to bring in the additional revenue.

I've witnessed firsthand boards that collectively roll up their sleeves and take action. The wrong action! They slash away at expenses ... and undercut their mission.

That's what happened at the New York Public Library a few years back. The city and state had severely curtailed its allocations, cutting the Library's revenue in half. And to make matters worse, the fundraising program was stalled.

The president of the Library eliminated staff and opened fewer hours each day. When that didn't save enough, he closed the Library two days a week. Then three. After that, he closed branches.

Enter Vartan Gregorian, the new president. With a blend of charm and persistence, he mobilized the board and gave them marching orders. He made them understand their role was to give (and to give plenty!) and to ask others for support.

Within two years, the situation was turned around. And to this day the New York Public Library flourishes.

For trustees to allow a mission deficit is unpardonable, an abdication of the trust placed in them as board members. When this happens, you can hear the dull clang of the organization's death knoll.

Sacred Heart Hospital in Eugene, Oregon is one of the largest medical centers in the Northwest. I was at a meeting of the board a while back.

The debate was heated. There was a financial crisis. The board was split down the middle.

Should they severely cut programs? Eliminate free services? Discontinue their extensive outreach programs? Doing these things would surely save a lot.

Or should the board launch an intensive fundraising campaign requiring trustees to give more than they ever had, and to make a concerted effort to ask others to give. The debate seesawed.

I remember vividly what happened next.

"Sister, what do you suggest we do?" asked one board member.

Sister Veronica was the beloved president of the hospital. She stood. The room fell quiet. Sister spoke.

"No money, no mission."

That was all she said. But that was enough. Trustees voted unanimously and enthusiastically to proceed with raising the money to fund their mission-driven activities.

Remember Sister's admonition when you're tempted to emaciate your program. No money, no mission. Those four words say it all.

FAITH, FUN, FULFILLMENT

◆

Bonnie McElveen Hunter owns and manages a major corporation. But that's only part of her life.

She chairs the National Board of Governors of the American Red Cross. She's the most significant fundraiser nationally for the United Way. She's on the national board of Habitat for Humanity and involved in a dozen other activities. Add to all that, she's the former U.S. Ambassador to Finland.

"What drives you?" I ask Bonnie.

I want to find out why she's so involved in everything and how she ever finds the time.

"When I stand before God at the end of my life," Bonnie tells me, "I hope I don't have a bit of talent left. I want to be able to say, 'Lord, I used everything you gave me.'"

My hunch is you feel the same way, too. Serving as a trustee is your way of paying back. As Richard Antonini, (Cornerstone University in Grand Rapids, Michigan) told me: "It's the rent I pay for being on this earth."

It is an awesome responsibility you take on. You have accepted a sacred trust to sustain and increase the vitality of your organization. Because of you, the sick are healed, the abused are cared for, the hungry are fed.

You take this seriously because you know you make a difference. And those your organization serves bless you for all you do.

The French have a saying: *Tous Les Beaux Esprits Se Rencontrent*. Roughly translated it means that beautiful spirits seek each other out.

You have joined a noble army.

APPENDIX

GIVE YOURSELF A GRADE

It takes less than two minutes!

You volunteer your time. And that's darn precious. You may well ask: Isn't that good enough?

Well, no! Giving your time is plenty important. Your organization couldn't do its great work without you. But there's more.

That's why I've devised a report card. It covers every habit that's important to being an effective trustee.

Here's what I suggest. Review the items and score yourself. Determine whether there might be room for improvement. You want to be the best you can possibly be. To do anything less is to compromise the trust you hold for your organization.

Doing a self-appraisal is important, But what I think is better is to have a small committee (three or four) of the board evaluate each trustee once a year.

Well, yes, it may be difficult to tell a fellow truste he or she isn't living up to high expectations. It may seem like the Stations of the Cross, a burden to bear.

But who wants a board member who is ho-hum about the organization or is under-producing? Being a trustee is too prized a position for that. Thin gruel.

The next step can be tough. The Chair of the committee speaks with each trustee about his or her report card and where improvement is called for.

But don't wait for the committee to be formed in your organization. Complete the report card for yourself. Do it now. (I trust you to use the Honor System!)

BOARD MEMBER'S REPORT CARD

NAME _____

Grading Key:

Exemplary	5	Fair	2
Excellent	4	Not Sure	1
Very Good	3	Poor	0

GRADE

1) Board attendance (anything less than 70 percent attendance is a "2" or lower). _____

2) Participates at meetings (participates fully but doesn't dominate rates a "5"). _____

3) Understands the responsibility of board membership. _____

4) Prepares for board meetings. _____

5) Exercises good business judgment on behalf of the organization. _____

6) Pays particular attention to the quality of what the organization does. _____

7) Accepts fiduciary responsibility and is a thoughtful steward of funds. _____

8) Attends special activities (annual meetings, special events, retreats). _____

(Continued)

9) Has passion and commitment for the organization.   _____

10) Publicly advocates for the organization.   _____

11) Identifies men and women for gifts and board membership.   _____

12) Contributes financially to the full extent possible according to resources.   _____

13) Calls on others to give to the organization.   _____

14) Understands the importance of not allowing a "Mission Deficit."   _____

15) Limits the number of boards he or she serves on.   _____

TOTAL   _____

Scoring:

65 & above
You are an outstanding board member with the ability to accomplish much for the organization.

55 to 64
You demonstrate excellent dedication to your role as trustee.

45 to 54
The organization is fortunate to have you. Give attention to the areas that are lowering your score.

30 to 44
Some concern. Do you wish to continue serving?

Below 30
This is likely not the organization where you can bring a full measure of your passion and commitment.

ABOUT THE AUTHOR

Jerold Panas is among a small handful of the grand-masters of American fundraisers. This is his 10th book.

Jerry is considered one of the top writers in the field and a number of his books, including *Asking* and *Mega Gifts*, have achieved classic status.

Hailed by Newsweek as "the Robert Schuller of fundraising," Jerry is a popular columnist for Contributions magazine and a favorite speaker at conferences and workshops throughout the nation.

He is executive director of one of the premier firms in America and is co-founder of the Institute for Charitable Giving. The very term "philanthropy" would mean less without Jerry's influence.

He lives with his wife, Felicity, in a 1710 farmhouse in northwest Connecticut.

A Classic • Also by Jerold Panas

ASKING

**A 59-Minute Guide to Everything Board Members,
Volunteers, & Staff Must Know to Secure the Gift**
by Jerold Panas, 112 pp. $24.95

It ranks right up there with public speaking. Nearly all of us fear it. And yet it is critical to our success. Asking for money. It makes even the stout-hearted quiver.

But now comes a book, *Asking: A 59-Minute Guide to Everything Board Members, Staff and Volunteers Must Know to Secure the Gift.* And short of a medical elixir, it's the next best thing for emboldening staff, board members and volunteers to ask with skill, finesse ... and powerful results.

Jerold Panas, who as a consultant, board member and volunteer has secured gifts ranging from $50 to $50 million, understands the art of asking better than anyone in America.

He knows what makes donors tick, he's intimately familiar with the anxieties of board members, and he fully understands the frustrations and exigencies of staff.

He has harnessed all of this knowledge and experience and produced a landmark book.

What *Asking* convincingly shows – and one reason staff applaud the book and board members devour it – is that it doesn't take stellar sales skills to be an effective asker. Nearly everyone, regardless of their persuasive ability, can become an effective fundraiser if they follow a few step-by-step guidelines.

You have to know your cause, of course, and be committed to it. But, nearly as important, you have to know how to get the appointment, how to present your case, how to read your donor's words, how to handle objections, how to phrase your request, and even what behaviors to avoid.

Panas mines all of this territory, and because he speaks directly from his heart to the heart of board members, staff, and volunteers, the advice is authentic, credible, and ultimately inspiring.

Emerson & Church, Publishers

The Gold Standard in Books for Your Board

Each can be read in an hour • Quantity discounts up to 50 percent

Fund Raising Realities Every Board Member Must Face
David Lansdowne, 112 pp., $24.95, ISBN 1889102105

More than 50,000 board members and development officers have used this book to help them raise substantial money – in sluggish and robust economies. Have your board spend just *one* hour with this classic and they'll come to understand virtually everything they need to know about raising big gifts.

Asking   Jerold Panas, 112 pp., $24.95, ISBN 1889102172

It ranks right up there with public speaking. Nearly all of us fear it. And yet it's critical to our success. *Asking for money.* This landmark book convincingly shows that nearly everyone, regardless of their persuasive ability, can become an effective fundraiser if they follow Jerold Panas' step-by-step guidelines.

The Ultimate Board Member's Book
Kay Sprinkel Grace, 120 pp., $24.95, ISBN 1889102180

A book for *all* nonprofit boards: those wanting to operate with maximum effectiveness, those needing to clarify exactly what their job is, and, those wanting to ensure that all members are 'on the same page.' It's all here in jargon-free language: how boards work, what the job entails, the time commitment, the role of staff, effective recruiting, de-enlisting board members, and more.

Fund Raising Mistakes that Bedevil All Boards (& Staff Too)
Kay Sprinkel Grace, 112 pp., $24.95, ISBN 1889102229

There's no excuse for making a fundraising mistake anymore. And that goes for board members, staff, novice, or veteran. If you blunder from now on, it's simply evidence you haven't read Kay Sprinkel Grace's book, in which she exposes *all* of the costly errors – 40 in total – that thwart us time and again.

How Are We Doing?   Gayle Gifford, 120 pp., $24.95, ISBN 1889102237

Until now, almost all books dealing with board evaluation have had an air of unreality about them. The perplexing graphs, the matrix boxes, the overlong questionnaires. Enter Gayle Gifford, who has pioneered an elegantly simple way for your board to evaluate and improve its overall performance. It all comes down to answering a host of simple, straightforward questions.

Big Gifts for Small Groups
Andy Robinson, 112 pp., $24.95, ISBN 1889102210

If yours is among the thousands of organizations for whom six- and seven-figure gifts are unattainable, then in this book you'll learn everything you need to know to secure big gifts: how to get ready for the campaign, whom to approach; how to ask; what to do once you have the commitment; even how to convey your thanks in a memorable way.

Emerson & Church, Publishers

Copies of this and other books from the publisher
are available at discount when purchased
in quantity for boards of directors or staff.

Emerson
& Church
PUBLISHERS

P.O. Box 338 • Medfield, MA 02052
508-359-0019 • www.emersonandchurch.com